MARCH 2022

AN ANTHOLOGY OF ARTICLES

BRAIN BOOSTER ARTICLES

Contents

Preface

"Start writing, no matter what. The water does not flow until the faucet is turned on".

-Louis L'Amour

This book is a bouquet of articles contributed by students, professors and academicians. Hundreds of students and professors are contributing their work to Brain Booster Articles, we are here to provide ample information about Law and Contemporary issues. Our aim is to provide a platform for today's generation to express their views and ideas on law and contemporary law.

CHAPTER ONE

SOCIAL JUSTICE AND GENDER EQUALITY

Author: Sneha Nandi, V year, Law College Durgapur

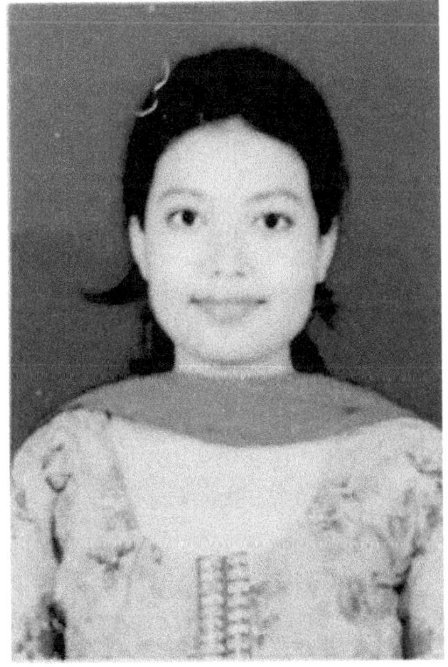

Co-author: Pritam Ghosh, V year, Law College Durgapur

<u>Abstract</u>

Gender Equality, if we interpret the words, it means equal treatment towards every gender. Justice should be done to all individuals irrespective of their gender, whether it is female, male or third gender. We often talk about gender equality for bringing equal rights to the women and there are groups and NGOs also who fights for the rights and welfare of women. In recent times several rights are given to the third gender which was not previously existed in our system. But what about men? Are they getting every right? This area needs some light. Though it is true that women need more protection as most of the time they are being harassed, raped, being murdered for dowry etc. and there are several laws to protect them. But men are suffering too. Many men are the victim of Domestic violence, many false cases are being made against men; especially for getting divorce and to claim maintenance, men are also being raped. There are no such laws to protect men. The laws of ours in some extents are gender biased we should say. There are beliefs like men can't be a victim in such kinds of violence just because they are presumed to be stronger physically, another is only a female can be a rape victim and only a male can be rapist. In the world several cases are occurring but they are unreported by the media or other things due to these stereotypical beliefs. Article 14 of the constitution provides for equal protection of law. So, there should be laws to protect everybody and not to a particular gender. A law is made when there is a need of that in the society and it is the high time to make laws for men as well. Society needs to be aware of the fact that men are being victimized too.

Introduction

"Injustice anywhere is threat to justice everywhere"

We often hear this quote. Especially at the times when any injustice takes place to a woman. It is very often that we see news of 'rape', 'dowry death', and 'cases of domestic violence' in newspapers. Thus, when we hear about any injustice, we create a picture in our mind that it is happening to a woman. Though our constitution guarantees the 'equality before law' under Article 14, whenever we talk about gender equality, the first thing that comes into our mind that women are being deprived of their rights, they are being tortured, raped etc. Maybe it is because of the phase 'gender inequality', which has been used for women only but the impact of it on men has not been addressed ever. There is a stereotypical belief that violence cannot be made to a man, as they are physically stronger than other genders. Generally, men who faces violence are ashamed of what will people say. There is a fear of being judged by people. And they don't want to face legal consequences because of gender biasness. As most of the laws are in favor of women, they fear that they will lose the case. Often men don't talk about violence in thinking of their family, their children. They think it will cause unnecessary nuisance to their family. But we really need to focus on the issues that violence against men is also happening though the number of it is still lower than the cases of women, but it is happening. Men are being harassed by false cases. False rape cases, misuse of section 498A of the Indian Penal Code etc. are so easy to send a man behind the bars. And the duration it takes to prove that he is not guilty, can ruin his entire life. So, we need gender neutral laws which will treat every gender equally.

False cases Against Men

A few years ago, voice raised saying '#Meetoo' to protect women who are being harassed in work place, seeing the present condition how men are being harassed of false allegations brought against them. #Mentoo should also be started to protect the interest of the men

It has been claimed that 51% of the suicides between men who are accused of sexual assault were due to false allegations brought against them.[1] "In 2019 a protest was being held at The India Gate, New Delhi, demanding justice for men facing unsubstantiated accusation of sexual assault. The demonstrators referred the recent case involving The Chief Justice of India, plan to start a movement called #mentoo and also demanded that the identifying of the accused men be kept swaddle until all legal proceedings were concluded. In a case after 2 years the POCSO special court observes that the accused is not guilty of the rape charges brought against him, but the accused already spent 2 years in jail. This is how men are being harassed and judged. Just because laws against rape protect the interest of women, it does not mean men can be harassed easily. A 47- year-old uncle of a 16 years old girl was acquitted on charges of raping her and getting her pregnant, the court observes that the victim's conduct cannot be relied on. The girl named her uncle after a failed abortion left her bleeding. After 2 years the court finds that there is a boy who is very close to the girl and has also helped girl to have abortion pills and they have hidden their 'Love Relationship'. The court while acquitting the accused stated that there was excessive delay in lodging First Information Report and the reason given has not been explained properly. The evidences presented before the court was not appropriate and considerable.

On 22nd August 2021 Delhi High Court expresses worry over ' alarming increase' of false rape cases. Justice SubramanianPrasad made the observation while rejecting a plea seeking to quash a First Information Report for offence of rape, in which the parties pleaded that they had easily settled the matter and entered into a compromise. The court also pointed out that the parties had registered cross- cases against each other for offences under section 376(rape) of the Indian Penal Code at the AmanVihar police station, Delhi. In this present case it seems that both the party has filed cases among each other without having sensitivity to the offences of rape and also says that cases of rape should not be reported as false to settle personal anger.

False rape allegation has the potential to damage the career and life of the accused. The accused in a false rape case losses his prestige and cannot face his family and is condemned for life. Undoubtedly women face pain of abuse but now a days men are also not very far away in getting victimized against false Cases of dowry. Many a times it has been found that for settling private greed between the spouse, false cases of dowry have been filed where the groom and the family of the groom is being tortured and being harassed. For prevention of dowry government has introduced an act named The Dowry Prohibition Act 1961, section 3 of such act provides penalty for giving and taking of dowry, meanwhile many people are misusing the section of such act where any property or stridhan given in mutual consent during marriage to the bridegroom as a gift by the bride's family. After some months or years due to some greediness the bride or the family of the bride files a false complain just to harass the groom's family. Saying such property has been acquired as dowry by the groom's family.

In the case of Rajender Bhardwaj vs Mrs. Anita Sharma (Delhi High Court 1992)

The fact of the case was that there was a question to the context that the allegations brought against the husband by his wife was that Rupees 35000/- was demanded for construction and Rupees 9000/- for scooter are true or false? They were found false by the court. In this case it was also found that the sister and mother of the men were also being harassed and accused for false dowry case. Thus, they are the examples how men are being tortured, just to settle personal greed this type of false cases are being filed. On the 1ˢᵗ April 1990 a couple got married and started to stay together, everything going in their life was very good after 5-6 months of their marriage the wife started quarrelling and threatening the husband and mother-in- law, seeing this the husband rented a separate property, but still the wife's difference in opinion didn't stop. After some days the wife was found to have interest in the property of the in-laws and wanted to sell it and get the portion of money from the sale. For settling her greed, she filed a false dowry and harassment case and till the court acquainted the husband and the mother- in- law they were being harassed.

Domestic Violence: The punishment for domestic violence only given to men and their family. As there is a stereotypical belief that as men are physically more powerful than women, violence can't be made to them. But the study shows 52.4% men among 1000 married men in Haryana, between the age group of 21- 49, face gender- based violence in the hands of their wives or intimate partners. The definition of domestic violence includes both physical and mental violence. According to the study 3.4% - 20.3% male is victim of physical violence and 10.6%- 40% is victim of some other sorts of violence[2]. But there are no punishments for violence against men, that means no protections are provided to men to protect them from violence.

Section 498 A was inserted in the IPC with a view to provide a shield to women from cruelty and harassment in marital relationship. Now a days we can see the increasing number of false domestic violence cases. As section 498 A of the Indian Penal Code is a ground for claiming divorce and alimony, several false cases are being filed to get divorce easily. And the allegation under section 498A is so serious that it is too easy to put a man behind the bars. An allegation under this section can ruin a man's whole life.

<u>Anju vs. Government of NCT of Delhi</u>

A wife challenged the lower courts order in Bombay High Court, where the husband got discharged from the charges under section 498 A of IPC against him. The Bombay High Court by observing that no time, date, places, month or year are mentioned, when she was subjected to be tortured. It concluded that the order of the lower court has not made any mistake, as it noted the allegations against the respondent were fairly general, untrue, and unspecific.

<u>Other violence</u>

The act of rape is thought to be a crime towards women. According to the definition of 'rape' in India rape is an act of penile penetration, or any other object without the consent of a woman under section 375 of Indian Penal Code. But some males are rape victim too. They are being raped too. 1 in 6 men are being suffered from sexual abuse and assault. In India there is no cases reported. 1in 71 men are being raped in United States[3].

Few days back, in Pakistan a male rape case came in frontline. Where a 14- year boy, named Jamal was raped and murdered by Nasir. It was reported by a non- governmental organization WAR (War Against Rape). This is just an instance. Similar kinds of thing are happening worldwide.

Stalking is another type of violence the definition of which under IPC states it is a crime against woman only under section 354D (1). But stalking happens against male also. According to National Statistics Domestic Violence 43.5% men are being stalked by their intimate partner.

Injustice towards men: In India, the laws protect a woman more as the rate of crime against women are greater in number. And it is the need of the society for the safety of women. But the rights given to protect a woman, they are often misused. An accused is innocent until proven guilty. Is it really true? The answer is no. When any incident arises between a man and a woman. Before knowing the fact of the case, the society assumes that the man is guilty and the woman is victim.

Sarvjeet Singh Case

In 2015, Sarvjeet Singh was accused of harassing a lady, named Jasleen Kaur. She clicked some pictures of him, when she was asked why she is taking pictures. She replied that police will be at his residence. After that Jasleen took her social media account to raise the issue in public and stated she was harassed by Sarvjeet Singh Bedi. A rush has been created. Some news channels started to name him as 'Delhi's Pervert'. A case was filed against him under section 354A and 502 of Indian Penal Code. He lost his Job. His life was ruined just by one post by Jasleen Kaur. During the trial Jasleen was absent in 14 hearings, that is duration of 3 years. Later some videos of the actual incidents were posted by the witnesses, who were present at the spot. And Sarvjeet Singh Bedi has proved innocent in 2018.

By this incident we can see that, it is so easy to ruin a man's life by false allegations like this. There are several cases of women misusing the protections given to them by law, which are happening on a daily basis but are unreported. This is not gender equality rather it is injustice to a particular gender.

Worldwide rates of violence against men

Not only in India, this is the scenario of the entire world. According to American Journal of Emergency Medicine, the cases of domestic violence has increased globally by 22% to 30% at the time of covid-19 pandemic. The National Coalition Against Domestic Violence reports 1 in 9 men experience violence by their intimate partners in United States. The National Statistics Domestic Violence states 1 in 4 men experience physical abuse by their wives or intimate partners. And 1 in every 71 men in United states are being raped[4]. So, the cases of violence against men are not zero. Though it is not same as the number of women, it is there and men are facing it too.

Suggestions

1. False Rape cases- When A rape case is being found by a court as false, courts may take Suo - moto steps to punish such person bringing the false allegations. false rape allegations have potential to destroy a man's mental as well as social conditions. And there should also be a checks and balances under section 376 of Indian penal code 1860 where people should be aware that filling this case just to for some personal grave is not cool. It may destroy the life of the man against whom such false allegations have been brought.

2. Men are also being harassed by women, many a times it has been recorded that to settle personal grave, men are being harassed awarding with blackmail and cases registered under section 498a of the Indian penal code 1860, courts may take Suo – moto steps to protect the interest of the

men against whom such false cases have been Registered. Which will aware and help in prevention of cases which are being filled falsely to harass men.

3. As section 375 of the Indian penal code 1860 says a rape can only be committed to women by men in different ways as said in the act. There is no scope for adult male victim. Men are also being raped and abused. The rape laws should also be made for men to protect the interest of the men. Men should also be aware and without hiding move ahead to file a complaint and society also shall accept these things normally.

4. Section 354D of the Indian penal code 1860 says stalking done by men is punishable but there is no scope for the victim males who are being stalked and harassed like the women are, neither there is any legislation which can safeguard and protect the interest of men.

5. As we know the Government has introduced an Act named, Dowry Prohibition Act, 1961, to prevent taking and giving of dowry, but the number of false cases is increasing day by day. Men and their families are suffering for false allegations against them. So, there should be some provisions to protect them against the malicious intentions. This may help in decreasing the number of such cases.

6. Sections such as 375, 354A, 354D, 498A of the Indian Penal Code 1860 and the provisions of Dowry Prohibition Act are very sensitive in nature. False cases registered under these sections has potential to finish the entire life of a person. Thus, when such allegations are proven to be false the court should take Suo- moto cognizance to punish such person, who made those false allegations. This will promote awareness that just to satisfy personal greed these cases cannot be filed.

Conclusion

Now a day in this modern era, there is no difference between men and women lifestyles. Previously men used to protect their families but now both are equal both have equal capability to work and they equally manage family. Thus, if a woman can come so far from a position where they were not allowed to do many things, why not men can open up about them? Only if they can open up about that they are suffering too, the society will be aware of the fact and will accept it. The struggles of men should be focused. Laws are needed for the protection of men against this malice intentions. And the Judiciary is the only hope, who can put lights on these matters. So that the legislature put some attention on making laws for the protection of men.

The Constitution provides equality before law but there is no such provision or acts which will safeguard the interest of the men. But we all can hope that looking at the present condition the legislature may take several steps to protect the interest of the men too.

[1]#MenToo: Protect men against false allegations, say Delhi protesters | Delhi News - Times of India (indiatimes.com) last retrieved at 04.00PM 18.02.2022 [2]A Cross-sectional Study of Gender-Based Violence against Men in the Rural Area of Haryana, India (nih.gov) [3]Statistics (ncadv.org) [4]Statistics (ncadv.org)

CHAPTER TWO

THE ADDICTED BRAIN

Author: Supriya Garhwal, I year of B.A.,LL.B. from Gujarat National Law University

ABSTRACT

Drug addiction and usage are important public and social health problems that impact individuals everywhere in this world. There are still gaps in our understanding of the factors that make a contribution to drug misuse, despite significant progress. On the other hand, drug abuse and addiction are widely known to get a multifactorial etiology. The significance of social factors in the initiation and maintenance of drug use, abuse, and addiction will be examined in this study, with an emphasis on the influence of peer groups, family, living environment and groups. According to the report, creating effective intervention tactics in this field necessitates a thorough understanding of the causes of drug abuse and addiction. The study focuses on the relevance of society in assisting people in overcoming drug addiction.

INTRODUCTION

Drug addiction is a fascinating and essential issue that has its roots in brain function. In the psychological and social context, the drug is a word for a daily regimen substance which directly acts on the brain or nervous system. I define addiction as a pattern of conduct that causes distress, personal anguish, or has a bad effect on one's life. Taking a substance like methamphetamine frequently, for example, might lead to a feeling of compulsion to continue taking the drug despite its bad effects. The loss of a job, financial hardship, or health issues might all be bad consequences. The negative impact is a crucial element of addiction, according to many people. It should now be clear that not every repetitious action is detrimental to your life. Appropriate eating, for example, is a necessary yet repeated action. And it has no harmful consequences under typical conditions.In reality, the reverse is true. It has a beneficial effect.

There are a few more things that can happen when you engage in addictive behavior.Many people have tried and failed several times to cease their habit. To have the same impact, they may have tried increasing the frequency of the activity or the medication dose. They may also discover that when they stop doing the activity or taking the substance, they begin to feel awful and enter a withdrawal state, prompting them to resume using the drug to escape the agony of withdrawal.

DRUGS AND MEDICINES

A curative and beneficial chemical, such as an antibiotic or an antidepressant, is referred to as medicine. A substance can be both a drug and a medication at times. Amphetamine, for example, may be used as a pharmaceutical to treat ADHD or as a narcotic that is misused and addicted.

Alcohol, nicotine, marijuana, some prescription drugs, methamphetamine, cocaine, and other addictive substances include alcohol, nicotine, marijuana, certain prescription drugs, methamphetamine, cocaine, and others. Because medications are so harmful, we must conduct research on them using animals. We could not have learnt as much about drugs or developed the treatments that are available for addicts without the accessibility and proper usage of animals.

When big groups of addicts are compared to large groups of non-addicts, it becomes clear that the addicts have some personal features and environmental elements in common. Of course, if you're struggling with drugs or other addictions, you should get help immediately. While some people can simply quit using drugs, others cannot. We have no idea why.

Some people require therapy in order to remain drug-free. The essential thing to remember is that therapy is effective. It will help if you get the correct therapy.

More than 80% of persons aged 12 and above have used alcohol at some point in their lives. Other drugs have varying percentages that eventually decrease.Only a small percentage of people have taken heroin at some point in their lives. Medicine expenses are far higher than most people believe. Illegal drugs are expected to cost society around $180 billion per year, alcohol is roughly the same, and tobacco is about the same or slightly higher.

We don't have a precise metric for calculating suffering, but we do know what occurs. We've all heard stories about folks whose lives were nearly ruined by drugs. Our confidence, perspective, and performance are all harmed when we are emotionally beaten by intense drug impulses, or anything else for that matter. Some individuals lose their jobs, their loved ones, their friends, and their personal and financial assets. Some folks lose all they own. Some people end up in court for divorce. Also, due to pharmacological side effects and toxicity, there is a drastic and considerable loss of health. Problems arise when people's health is disregarded, such as when addicts are consumed while getting and consuming drugs.

Some medications drastically alter your life and have disastrous health implications. We frequently hear people state that they are hooked to specific foods or that they are addicted to a certain television series.Various addictions have been documented in literature.

ADDICTION OF GAMBLING

It must be convincingly established that certain people's conduct resembles that of a brain illness or addiction. At the present moment, there is sufficient evidence to classify gambling as an addiction condition. And it is probable that more evidence will emerge in the future, and some other behaviors may be classified as addictions, necessitating treatment for certain people. It has been demonstrated that gambling may be a persistent activity that leads to harmful effects.

Of course, one of the negative consequences might be a financial loss that prevents you from meeting your commitments, such as paying your rent or purchasing food for your family. There are some more traits, in addition to gambling away money that you require. For example, you haven't been able to cut back or stop, and attempting to do so causes you worry. You may lie about how much you gamble or attempt to hide it, and you may gamble after stressful situations. You may be able to stop gambling for a period of time, but you will relapse, just as with other addictions. There are people who behave in this way and benefit from treatment, according to studies.

In terms of the causes of drug addiction, sociological theory says that people become drug addicts as a result of their circumstances or social environment. Sutherland's Differential Association Theory characterizes drug use as a taught habit, most commonly in small intimate groups. According to the social learning theory (Akers & Burgess), drug dependency conditioned learning and reinforcement comes through connection with others who define drug use positively. The Strain hypothesis is concerned with the severe strain placed on individuals, which drives them to break from internalized standards. Drug misuse is seen as an aberrant habit in India, and drug users and addicts are seen as aberrant individuals who, unlike non-conformists, are not interested in improving societal conditions or aiding mankind.

Addiction is caused by a mix of genetics and psychological events. More specifically, we'd want to address some of the societal reasons, as well as how social problems are linked to people. The site of residence, how society views the individual, and how the individual views society some are caused by the person's incorrect perspective, while others are genuine.

The kind of influence of parents, imposition of discipline over the children, the parents' involvement in their children's future career prospects, and parents remaining aware of their obligations towards their children have all been identified as important factors that influence children's decision to enter the drug world. Family members' drinking/ smoking and drug-taking habits also have an impact on drug usage.

CASE STUDY

An 18-year-old teenager was discovered seriously addicted to narcotics. He came from a working-class background with both parents employed. The parents were educated up to the intermediate level. The parents' sole goal was to educate their only kid. They were, however, unaware that the children's capacities differed from one another. Because of his poor academic performance, the youngster was often beaten, punished, and scolded. They used to make comparisons between him and the boys who were doing well in school. This experience bothered the child to the point where he told one of his friends, who was also struggling academically. Both of the pals attempted to escape the uncomfortable conditions in which they found themselves at home. They happened to run across one of their friends who used to do drugs. They began using drugs on the instruction of the third friend. The drug's dose was gradually increased, and some of the psychological instability became apparent. He was taken to the clinic on the doctor's instruction. The parents were completely unaware of their error and their son's terrible condition.

In this matter we can clearly see that it was the pressure of exceling in studies which forced the children to take drugs in order to relive their tension, which at a later stage became addiction. So the support and understanding of parents play a vital role in helping their child to stay away from drugs or even if he started having drugs to stop them.

<u>THEORIES OF DRUG USE</u>

A large variety of hypotheses have been developed in the field of drug use research to explain or account for drug use.

1. Control of the environment

According to social control theory, deviations of societal standards are normal, comprehensible, and do not require an explanation. Its proponents claim that what has to be addressed is why people adapt to societal standards. If we were left to our own to do whatever we want , we would all of course breach the law and will engage in various criminal activities and normative offenses.Attachment (or "bonds") to conventional persons, ideas, organizations, and activities, they claim, explains that we have to follow a conduct which will be law- abided and conformance to norms prevailing in the society. We don't want to jeopardize or undermine our "investment" in oureducation,parents, marriage, a legal profession, or conventional religion by indulging in illegal acts, which includes illicit, drug use. As a result, we detect the following models in drug usage: teenagers with college plans or who are married, religious and/or have children are less likely to consume drugs, whereas those without these ambitions are more likely to consume drugs.

2. Self-Control

Self-control theory argues that it is affinity , not normative infractions or criminal activity, that has to be explained. However, its explanation is somewhat different, tracing its main element all the way back to childhood. Low self-control, according to self-control theory, is the element that accounts for deviance and criminality, including drug usage. Weak, ineffective parenting is the answer to the issue of what causes poor self-control. Children who grow up in an atmosphere where their parents are unwilling or unable to praepostor and regulate their disordered conduct develop a pattern of high-risk,impulsive, hedonistic and, eventually, short-term, gratifying behavior, which includes criminality and drug addiction.People that lack self-control tend to beirresponsible, thoughtless,insensitive, self-centered, nonverbal,short-sighted, inconsiderate, intolerant of frustration, and pleasure focused. Cheaters, thieves, Grabbers, liars, and exploiters are what they are. They behave without regard for the long-term implications of their conduct. Drug use is only one of many symptoms of their attitude toward life, which is to do whatever you want, whenever you feel like it, regardless of whether it harms others or, in the long run, harms yourself.

3. Social learning

People are not "naturally" put at a risk to consume drugs or commit crimes, according to social learning theory; instead, they must learn the positive value of non-normative actions. The theory of differential association is the first social version of learning. It pertains primarily to crime and hence is known as the theory of differential association. According to learning theory, children form differential attachments to choose social circles that give "social contexts for exposure" to definitions of acceptable and improper conduct, role models to copy, and chances to engage in certain behaviors. Drug usage may be discouraged or encouraged in these settings.

4. Conflict

According to conflict theory, inequality is the primary cause of drug usage, particularly serious, long-term misuse and reliance on "hard" substances like crack cocaine and heroin. Proponents of this idea say that domestic violence is significantly linked to social class, income, power, and neighborhood. Hard drug usage is substantially more common among lower- and working-class inner-city populations than among more wealthy sections of society. Drug selling is more likely to prevail in powerless,impoverished, socially unorganized groups than in more, structured and strong communities, according to the conflict viewpoint. Open, organized, and widespread drug trafficking is particularly likely if locals are unable to take any necessary political step to act against undesired undertakings among them.Furthermore, in communities where poverty is entrenched, the economic structure has never developed or has decayed and collapsed, and a sense of hopelessness, depression, and anomie is likely to take hold, making drug abuse particularly appealing and attractive, providing a means of "escape from a dreadful condition into one that appears, at least temporarily, more pleasant."

PREVENTION AND TREATMENT OF DRUGS

Drug addiction is to a large part to blame for current criminal conduct and moral deterioration. Unwin has stated that it is to blame for sexplosion. "Just as hippies brought depression, sexual freedom brings pornography, depravity, and obscenity." We must reverse the previous statements in order to avoid future drug addiction. Here are some tips for minimizing drug addiction.

1.The lower the odds of addiction, the stronger the social link: to strengthen the social bond (emotional, rote perception). Every day, for at least two hours, family members should sit and converse with each other, where everyone is free to share whatever he or she wishes, or whatever challenges they are facing.

2. Failure (in exams, in work, in marriage) should be accepted as a natural part of life. If the individual fails to meet his objectives, he must be treated with compassion. This will lessen the sting of failure and boost the ability to deal with adversity.

3. There are many stressors and strains in modern life. To relieve tension, the family must limit their objectives. As a result, the less the pressures, the fewer medications.

4. The kid should learn through his family that he is first and foremost a social being before becoming an individual, and that as a social person, he is responsible to others (parents, grandparents, brother, sister & other relations). This will boost both social commitment and social coercion. As a result, the stronger the social engagement and coercion, the lower the likelihood of drug usage.

5. Drug usage in recent years has surged among school students and slum inhabitants. Providing therapy to these adolescents who are experimenting with drugs will be an effective way to combat illegal drug usage.

6.Because the majority of drug users used drugs because of poor company from friends and family, parents must keep an eye on their children's pals' circles and relatives.

7. The government formed the Narcotic Intelligence Bureau and approved the Narcotic Drugs and Psychotropic Substance Act 1985 to combat drug trafficking. This statute stipulates that anyone implicated in drug trafficking shall be fined one lakh rupees and imprisoned for ten years. The penalty might be enhanced to 20 years in prison and a fine of up to two lakh rupees. A person who stores narcotics for illegal purposes

will face a fine, jail, or both. The court may also order that addict be sent to a rehabilitation institution for de-addiction treatment. The Indian government's Ministry of Welfare awards money to non-governmental organizations (NGOs) that seek to educate the public about drug addiction.

8. Parents should set a good example by abstaining from using illegal substances. The lower the level of deviance in the family, the lower the likelihood of addiction in the offspring.

9. India's Ministry of Welfare has devised a four-point action plan to combat drug usage. (1) Identifying, motivating, counselling, treating, and aftercare in the community; (2) raising awareness about the effects of drug misuse. (3) Provide training to service providers; (4) Assist non-profit organisations in implementing the programme by giving cash for the creation of counselling and de-addiction centres.

CONCLUSION

As a result, if the fundamental cause of drug addiction is stressful family events and terrible company from friends, it will be tough to treat patients unless and until they have a warm family atmosphere, love, and affection.

As a result, the two key components are strengthening the reliance and enhancing relationships. Many patients are either unable or unwilling to take on family responsibilities. Individuals become more aware of difficulties by participating in discussions about their position in the family in executing prescribed chores, developing good communication within the family, and sustaining family harmony and unity.

GENDER DISPARITY IN THE CRIMINAL JUSTICE SYSTEM OF INDIA

Author: Sandipa Bhattacharjee, IV year of B.A.,LL.B.(Hons.) from KIIT, SCHOOL OF LAW

<u>INTRODUCTION</u>

Discrimination of many types exists in our country. Discrimination is based on color, race, caste, sex, and other factors. Discrimination based on gender is not a new concept. Gender discrimination disadvantages women because they do not have equal possibilities as men, such as promotion in the workplace, independence, and so on.

Gender-based discrimination, according to the CEDAW Committee, is based on gender stereotypes, stigma, damaging and patriarchal cultural practices, and gender-based violence, all of which impede women's ability to access justice on an equal footing with men.[i]Discrimination between men and women exists not only in India but in many other countries as well. However, there is a significant gender disparity in terms of the number of times men and women serve in the criminal justice system.

Prosecutors and judges have distinct approaches to men and women accused of a crime when it comes to men they are considerably stricter than when it comes to women. Because the number of female criminals is lower, men must do more time in prison for the same offense. The arrests, pretrial treatment, and sentencing of female criminals are all influenced by racial disparities.[ii]

<u>GENDER DISPARITY IN SENTENCING</u>

Women are not inferior to men in today's world. They are excelling in all areas. However, there is some disadvantage that women frequently assist men in committing crimes. Women are now included as suspects, accused, and imprisoned in the criminal justice system.

The number of women in prison is steadily increasing. Judges may draw conclusions based on prejudices that may or may not be true when men and women commit the same type of crime. "Fair treatment does not entail treating everyone in the same way: it implies treating people equally in comparable situations," according to the UK's Equal Treatment Bench Book, published in 2013.[iii]

It is obvious that women receive lenient punishment, including non-payment of fines, when they commit crimes, because they must care for their children and families, and they are also weak to impose harsher penalties. As a result, women receive less penalty than men for the same crime. When it comes to property ownership, however, women are treated equally to males.

The Supreme Court delivered a landmark judgment in 1986, allowing women to seek an equal share of their father's property. In addition, prosecutors and judges in courts and tribunals must make adaptations for pregnant women to offer a safe atmosphere for them, and as a result, judges decide not to imprison them for a longer period.

Females were twice as likely as males to receive probation and were somewhat more likely than males to have their charges reduced, according to the researchers. In comparison to men, the total number of women sentenced to death is also quite low.[iv]The total number of women death penalty is also very small as compared to men. The overall death penalty is also very low in India. Supreme Court held that the death penalty should be given in 'rarest of rare cases only.[v]

PILLARS OF CRIMINAL JUSTICE SYSTEM & GENDER DISPARITY

Nearly all government institutions are patriarchal, which is the root cause and reason for sustaining all forms of gender discrimination. In India, veritably less chance of women working in government services. Historically, men have dominated regulatory institutions, which have favored men over women. Women's rejection leads to a lack of or slow growth, which unconsciously leads to weak policy perpetration and operation. Women were also barred from entering law-making institutions similar to parliament and statehouses, performing in manly dominance in the council. Women are unfit to engage in politics due to socio-artistic, profitable, and political factors. For a long time, women's domestic liabilities and limited domestic positions didn't give them sufficient liberty and commission to share in politics.

Women are underrepresented in the council, denying them the occasion to engage in the drafting of legislation. Women, who make up nearly half of the population of our nation, must debate, discuss, and agree on legislation before it can be legislated and followed.Judges who are women are also subordinated to misogyny. There have been cases of female advocates being blackened by male advocates. When a woman judge in Delhi's Karkardooma courts was subjected to sexual harassment by a prosecutor, she filed an FIR. Her chief judicial magistrate asked her to drop the case.[vi]

Various challenges are being faced by women in their lives. If women are a victim of any crime they generally don't get support from their families. They are being forced to shut themselves thinking about the reputation of the family, especially in the case of sexual assault or rape. In some cases, the women and their families are not aware of their legal rights as well. [vii]Women are also at risk if they are being arrested or convicted for any crime. Even the women are not allowed to be a witness in the cases because of their families.

CONCLUSION & SUGGESTION

There is a need for courts to stop using gender stereotypes when trying female offenders. The issue is not women's low crime rate, but sex-based behavioral segregation. Judges should apply a more neutral basis while taking into account other factors that drive women to commit crimes, rather than using their perception of a woman's role in society. However, there can't be a single criminal justice system for both male and female criminals because that would be only cosmetic fairness when they're still not on equal footing. Offenders with family members should be allowed some leeway; otherwise, their families will suffer as well.

However, this should be regulated to ensure that it does not go beyond the point of being unjust discrimination. To raise awareness about women criminals, some suggestions include simplifying bail procedures for women on trial, establishing more family courts to expedite case resolution, and recruiting more female judges to try cases involving women offenders to ensure a better understanding of the circumstances.

Author's Bio

I am Sandipa Bhattacharjee, a 4th-year B.A.LL.B (Hons.) student from KIIT Law School, Bhubaneswar. Researching & Writing have always been a passion for me. I am able to express my thoughts through my writing on different topics. This article will give the readers about the existing gender disparity in our criminal justice system & what all methods can be taken into consideration to curb this problem

CHAPTER FOUR

THE IMPACT OF GLOBALISATION AND LOSS OF CULTURAL IDENTITY

Author: Trishla Parihar, LLM Corporate and Commercial Law from School of Law, Christ University

<u>INTRODUCTION</u>

"Globalisation is a fact because of technology, because of the integrated global supply chain, because the change in transportation and we're not going to be able to build a wall around that."

-Barack Obama

Quoting Peter L. Berger "we also have a cultural phenomenon, the emergence of Global culture or of Cultural Globalisation". Globalization is a process of speedy growth and integration of countries. It happens through greater foreign trade and foreign investment. It is referred to increase the possibility for action between people in situations irrespective of geographical considerations as per the definition of social theorists. It is well-known thought that the world has become a "global village". The World is fusionism and expanding the blanket fold areas of culture as result food habits, dress habits, lifestyle and views are being internationalized. Globalisation has a positive impact and negative impact on the social and cultural values in India. Globalisation has created a new World in itself by providing ease to people's life. by opening a new corridor of employment. It has also made inroads in the cultural heritage of this country. Globalisation is not a one day progress it is a movement towards economic, political and cultural modernization, taken by the state in India. It is accepted by people with an enhanced sense of self-consciousness and awareness of identity. Cultural modernization is a phenomenon that is accepted by the people and sponsored by the forces of globalization, it is resented or restructured. The reformation in the core cultural value, its language, social practices and styles of life is the utmost important situation.

The vigour sense of self-awareness generated among the members of the local cultures and communities to raise the level of awareness is so needed to succeed in making adaptive reconciliation with the forces of globalization. There is a linkage between both visible and invisibility. The linkages are both visible and invisible, it is defining the cultural interdependence, the cultural identity and the cultural values among the communities and regions in India which have existed. Historically, it is clashing with the spirit of the national identity. These bonds seem to become stronger as India encounters the forces of modernization and globalization. India is rich in cultural fusion and it has vast diversification of cultural identity. The Tribal culture has its specified culture which is respected not just by other communities but has been given unique identification by the government to preserve the Tribal values and omnificent culture. The land of India is considered as a VasudhaivKutumbukam (वसुधैवकुटुम्बकम्) that is, the Earth is a family. It is inculcated from pre-education to respect the cultural diversification and cultural fusion of the Country. Although cultural fusion is broadened aspect of psychological acts of a person Globalisation has affected the idea of diversification of culture which has led to a decline in the respect of that particular gene of the culture. It stabilises. The culture is a shared idea among the group of people that is surrounded by a place of birth, religion, language, cuisine, social behaviour, art, literature, music etc. Some cultures are expanded having enormous ideology attached to it. There are others that are so connected with that ideology with the idea of culture. It is widespread, young, old, reflective, demonstrative where people are associated with that culture. Today, the treatment of cultural identity is getting impacted due to the evolvement of globalisation. It is getting regarded as a threat to the Country or the Countries. The speed to form a connection is increasing due to recent development in communication and globalisation.

Background: The History of Society's Secondary Memory

The cultural identity is very diversified, it is called cultural identity because it is rooted deep since the evolution of the culture in the environment. Today, technology and other societal norms are creating connections to globalise the World with diversified cultures. Human activities are challenged and integrated into worldwide networking zone. The Globalised economy is speeding up the social and cultural identity and integrating into a larger network of systems. The process of cultural fusion is more like trade immigration, the immigration of ideas is known as the Globalisation of cultural identity. Initially, the knowledge of the culture has developed through the human lives, their imagination and it is structured primarily by local geography and topology and religion. Before, two hundred years ago, every minute of human evolutionary time was moulded by the local identical culture and the economic criteria. Prior to the development of the situation of a villager (at that time village only exists), they read, study, work, learn, reproduce, and bury all being in the same place or same village. Also termed to be the place from time till death. similarly, the culture of the tribal society has been cultivating in the society, during the time of Narmada BachaoAndolan it was found that there is a tribal community called Bhil, Bhilara, Pavra, Tadvi are ethnic groups of Gujrat who they indulged in very famous for their painting. The Narmada project development has affected the lives of these tribes on the bank of Narmada. This became the story to bring in identity and the cultural crisis among various tribal communities based near Narmada. There are 163 varieties of tribal foods including mushrooms etc are found in the jungle which was once part of the Baiga diet and disappearing gradually. This includes millets as a part of the Baiga's diet now consumed as a medical need only. Every human being is a proud individual of the place he or she comes from, the heritage is an intrinsic part of it.

Respecting that heritage is because of the shared quality like the birthplace tradition etc. the cultural identity is originated from the non-Western third world since the end of the colonial period, and the Second World War contributed to some progress and undesired changes. Some of the most accepted phenomena were the weakening of extended family and acceptance of nuclear family. Development of a culture of both parents working to run the family. The migration from small to big cities in terms of employment and education drastically transformed the individual psychology. The thought of "we sense" is turned into "I self" These changes, family and individual psychology were structured by extended family, traditional Indian value system, and child-rising practices. Today, money is rotating in the market, women are enjoying an increased sense of independent self and working to increase their self-esteem. Nowadays, the Traditional Indian developmental stages may be spinning to more Western individualistic social structures. Additionally, we were also forced to give up some of the traditional and cherished values. This is reshaping the new self, a new sense of autonomy, and newer sense of individuation. Everything together contributing in the process of development of an evolving new culture, with hope of preparing us better for a new, better world.

Some Cultural identity are-

- Bula! This oft-used greeting in Fiji translates to "life," with its longer use ni sa bula Vinaka translating to "wishing you happiness and go...
- Explore of the Denish Heritage with peace and prosperity
- Italy has influenced cultures globally with its great achievements, from the Roman Empire to the Renaissance to the modern day.
- Preserving the culture of Tribal Community Globally.

Methodology

The research methodology undertaken in this study is doctrinal research as well as observational, it will be a research based on primary and secondary sources of data to be examined. The Primary sources are the information, rules, guidelines, decisions, and international legislations. Secondary sources like Scholarly Articles published in law journals, different case laws, government records, and various reliable online sources, news relating to marine bodies will also be relied upon. This is a qualitative research methodology.

Results

"The sea, the great unifier, is man's only hope. Now, as never before, the old phrase has a literal meaning: we are all in the same boat." quoted by Sir Jacques Yves Cousteau.

The culture is the universal sewer. As per the UN submission one on ten people are indulge in the cultural identity since it will directly or indirectly affect the market structure of particular company. On exploring the culture and using the source of the culture for their living. During the past decade the number of conventions has marked its way up, the only factor to consider is the effective use of these conventions. The laws that the Countries are framing for instance the Geographical Indication of the State, is that actually able to control the manipulation of un acceptable cultural identity? The US has laws with regards false cultural identity trading but the percentage of cases reported is not enough to consider the fact that the laws exist. The threats to cultural identity and cultural bodies and the diversity are many. The role of the international regime is to address all the factors that lead to pollution due to cultural identity, for instance submerge of the dharatal aacharan, pollution, and loss of habitat and its identity.

Conclusion

The Indian society is lot more changing because of the fact that there are lot of changes brought in the social culture. This cultural identity is giving a feeling of belonging to a group with similar characteristics. The following includes the idea of putting oneself, in someone's Nationality, ethnicity, beliefs and religion, social class or the part in which it is mention if you belong to a group that has his own culture. It is the way of life through expression of same feeling which you define yourself and add value to your social relationships. The Culture does not necessarily switch to the relation to economic and political circumstances. Culture is human psychological phenomena expands by itself. There are three stages for the popularizing the Cultural identity. The culture grows everyday and it is modified every day.

The first is relating to the human's life by producing goods and selling or exchanging them. The second explains the cultural activities to structure their relationships and build communities. The third stage stated that the way it is looked and motivate themselves to reach goals by following their beliefs and religion. Globalization is the flows of people, organizations, capital, images and ideas across the globe.

CHAPTER FIVE

IS UNIFORM CIVIL CODE: MERE RHETORIC?

Author: Md Ibaadur Rahman, I year of B.A.,LL.B.(Hons.) from Aligarh Muslim University

"The state shall endeavour to secure for the citizens a uniform civil code throughout the territory of India."- Article 44 of the Indian Constitution.

Introduction

To understand the concept of the Uniform Civil Code (hereinafter as UCC) we first need to dig deep into the structure of Indian Law, which can be broadly classified into 2 categories namely, Criminal Law and Civil Law.

Criminal laws of the country are secular and apply to all religious and tribal communities indiscriminately. Now considering the Civil laws, they are more than not, secular in nature, like the Law of Torts, Property laws, and Law of Contract. The only problem arises when considering the Family laws section of Civil Laws because every religious community has its laws in this regard. In India, we have different sets of Family laws for Muslims, Parsis, Christians, and Hindus (including Sikhs, Jains, and Buddhists).

The reasons put forward by the champions of UCC for its enforcement nationwide are: National integrity, Modernity, implementation of Secularism in its true sense, and removal of gender-unjust laws. [1]

PRE-INDEPENDENCE ERA AND MAKING OF THE CONSTITUTION

The will to have uniform laws was apparent from as early as the 1850's when Criminal laws were being made Uniform and Secular in nature. The only portion where non-uniformity was seen was in Family laws which deal with the matters of marriage, divorce, maintenance, adoption, inheritance, and succession.

When different laws of Hindus were being amended and gender-unjust laws were being abrogated during the 1930s,[2] the Muslim elite class pressurized for the passing of Islamic laws according to which Muslims throughout India would be dealt in matters of Family Laws. The Act is known as Muslim Personal Law (Shariat) Application Act, 1937.

In 1941, B.N. Rao Committee was set up to codify the Hindu laws to remove all gender-unjust laws and enact laws considering modernity, but unfortunately, it was only limited to only one community, i.e., Hindus, leaving other communities' laws untouched.

According to the recommendation of the Committee, Hindu Code Bills of the 1950s were passed and laws were enacted such as Hindu Marriage Act,1955, Hindu Succession Act, 1956, etc., However, the dream of B.R Ambedkar, the father of the Indian Constitution was left unfulfilled, mainly due to the communal atmosphere created due to large-scale blood-shedding during Partition. So, all in all, it was decided to incorporate the UCC in the Constitution under Article 44 enshrined in Part IV of the Constitution called Directive Principles of State Policy, as a directive medium for the future states to strive for.

POST INDEPENDENCE ERA AND THE RELEVANT CASES

UCC remained in the background till 1975 when suddenly the case of Mohd. Ahmed Khan v. Shah Bano Begum[3] once again brought the issue under the limelight. It was the case of maintenance, in which the divorced wife, Shah Bano, demanded maintenance under Section 125 of the CRPC, which is secular. The problem arose in front of the Supreme court when it was pointed out by the opposing counsel that the provision goes against the

Islamic Shariat Act, 1937 under which no maintenance was to be provided to a divorced woman.

The court ruled in favor of Shah Bano, and it was decided that the divorced woman is entitled to maintenance. The decision stirred row throughout the nation, particularly, All India Muslim Personal Law Board and further orthodox sections of Muslim society completely opposed the decision and under the pressurized environment, Rajiv Gandhi's government decided to pass the law called, Muslim Women (Protection of Rights on Divorce) Act, 1986.[4] This Act provided for the maintenance of a Divorced Muslim Woman, but only till the period of her iddat (3 lunar months after the pronouncement of divorce).

The legislation passed by Rajiv Gandhi's government was further challenged and its Constitutionality was questioned in the case of Danial Latifi v. Union of India.[5] After interpreting the above-mentioned legislation, the Supreme Court stated that the maintenance needs to be provided to a woman even after the period of iddat, for which the husband has been provided with the period of 3 months to arrange for the money.

In 2017, we saw another landmark case dealing with Triple Talaq, called Shayara Bano v. Union of India,[6] which abrogated the Triple Talaq (Talaq-e-Biddat, i.e., pronouncing talaq 3 times at a single occurrence) declaring it as unconstitutional and against the women's rights.

REVIEW OF GOA'S CIVIL CODE

Though Goa's civil code is frequently cited as an example for applying the UCC throughout the nation. Especially after the remark of CJI Bobde in March 2021, there has been lots of discourse revolving around this topic.[7] On scrutinizing the Goa Civil code, one can be assured that it is not at all Uniform in nature and is biased towards Christian Community.

Some of the examples are:

Article 1057, Goa's Civil Code, which deals with marriage is patently non-uniform and has a different procedure of marriage registration for Catholics and non-Catholics.

Article 1204, Goa's Civil Code, which deals with divorce is another example of gender-unjust laws, according to which man can get a divorce if a wife commits adultery, but the wife can get a divorce only when the husband keeps a mistress in the conjugal home or abandons her.

Article 3 of the Decree of Gentile Hindu Usages and Customs of Goa, 1880 provides for the bigamy, viz., a husband can have a second wife if the first one fails to deliver a child by the age of 25, or fails to provide a male issue by the age of 30.

SUPREME COURT'S JUDICIAL ACTIVISM IN THIS REGARD

Supreme Court has been provided with the power of judicial activism under Article 142 of the Constitution. Although the Court has been quite active in all areas of law, in the case of UCC, it appears to rely on a mere rhetorical approach, in the meanwhile exerting the legislature to draft the law for the same.

The other possible reason for SC's rhetoric approach could be the recent trend across the globe in favour of acceptance of legal pluralism.[8] As to sum it up, we can say that Supreme Court as the guardian of the Constitution advocates for the UCC but deep down accepts the recent trends and reality and is keener towards a pragmatic approach for solving this problem.

CONCLUSION

The laws in India are quite uniform baring Family laws, so what we need is 'Uniform Family Laws'. We need to balance the aim of valuing and preserving the rich heritage of composite culture along with the renunciation of practices that are derogatory to women's dignity as mentioned in Article 51A(f) and Article 51A(e) of the Constitution respectively.

There are 2 possible ways of doing it; one by drafting a common civil law applicable to all religious and cultural societies, which would be all-encompassing legislation. The other model is a piecemeal abrogation of gender-unjust and unconstitutional laws. The latter one despite being a slow process is more guarantying and better-sounding for maintaining integrity throughout the nation as has been demonstrated through the case of Shayara Bano. The piecemeal approach will further ease the task of the Judiciary in assimilating the different personal laws and can be further supplemented alongside a 'within-the-community-change' which will further reduce the friction.

Author's Bio

I AM A FIRST-YEAR STUDENT OF BALLB, CURRENTLY IN THE 1ST SEMESTER, KEENLY INTERESTED IN WRITING ON CONSTITUTIONAL AND RECENT LEGAL TRENDS, A BIBLIOPHILE FOR SURE.

CHAPTER SIX

K. S. PUTTASWAMY v. UNION OF INDIA

Author: Mansi Singh, V year of B.A.,LL.B. from Gitarattan International Business School (Affiliated to Guru Gobind Singh Indraprastha University)

BACKGROUND OF THE CASE

The Aadhaar project was initiated in 2009 to curb the problems of Duplicate ID documents. In 2008, the then Planning Commission decided to launch UIDAI (The Unique Identification Authority of India). Nandan Nilikani, CO Founder of Infosys appointed as its first Chairman.

The first 12-digit Aadhaar Number was issued on September 29, 2010. A biometric-based Unique Identity Number will be helpfulfor identification of eligible persons for Welfare schemes. It was considered as the most reliable proof of identity.

The project was initially launched as voluntary way of improving welfare service delivery but later in practice, the government made it mandatory for no. of services and forcing residents to sign up for Aadhaar to get access to things they were already due.

In 2016, Parliament Enacted The Aadhaar Act 2016 to provide legislative backing to the project. This Act gave permission to use Aadhaar for authentication purposes by the Central and State government as well as private bodies and persons.

Government made Aadhaar mandatory for government projects such as LPG subsidies and mid-day meal scheme. In 2017, Parliament passed the Finance Act to amend the Income Tax Act, 1961 and made Aadhaar mandatory for filing Income Tax Returns and applying for PAN. In the meantime, Aadhaar bill was passed as money bill in the parliament. Since money bill does not need be introduce in Rajya Sabha but only in Lok Sabha, helped in passing of the Act. The Act was challenged in the Supreme Court.

The first petition was filed in 2012.

ISSUES RAISED

(1)Whether the Aadhaar project is unconstitutional on the ground that it creates a surveillance state?

The Supreme Court stated that Aadhaar does not tend to create any surveillance. It was held that since during the enrolment process, minimal biometric data in the form of iris and fingerprint is collected and UIDAI does not collect location or details, hence its purpose is blind. The information collected is minimal. The authentication process was not exposed to the internet. He authority also mandated using registered devices for authentication requests.

(2) What is the magnitude of Protection that need to be accorded to collection, Storage and usage of biometric data?

Sec 2(D) which pertains to Authentication Records, such records would not include Metadata as mentioned in Regulation 26(C) of the Aadhaar (Authentication) Regulations, 2016. Therefore, the above provision has been struck down by the court. One cannot store the data beyond the period of six months. Hence,Regulation 27 of Aadhaar (Authentication) Regulations, 2016 provides a data for a period of only five years.

(3) Whether the collection of Identity Data without Adequate Safeguards Interferes with the fundamental Right to Privacy Protected under Article 21 of the Constitution?

Violation of Right to Privacy cannot be granted in each and very matters involving individuals. Therefore, the matters involving a reasonable expectation of privacy will fall under the protection of Article 21.

The SC relied on the Triple Test.

(i) Existence of Law – Backed by the Statute (Aadhaar Act)

(ii) A Legitimate State Interest – To ensure that social benefit Schemes reach the deserving community.

(iii) Test of proportionality – Balances the professed benefits of Aadhaar and the potential threat it carries to the Fundamental Right to Privacy.

The SC held that third test has also been met as the purpose of the Act is to ensure Deserving Beneficiaries of welfare Schemes are correctly identified. It also achieves the balancing of two competing Fundamental Rights, Right to Privacy on the one hand and Right to food, Shelter and Employment on the other.

(4) Whether Aadhaar can be made mandatory for those Government Benefits and Services that citizens are entitled under the law?

The failure to establish identity of an individual has proved to be a major hindrance for successful implementation of those programmes. It was becoming difficult to ensure that subsidies, benefits and services reach the unintended beneficiaries.

(5) Does it violate a person's Fundamental Rights such as their Right to Practice any profession, Trade or Business and Right to Equality discriminates between individual and non-individual assesses.

It was held that it does no violates Fundamental Rights to Equality or the Fundamental Right to Practice one's Profession or Trade. Aadhaar is perceived as the Best Method of eliminating Duplicate PANs and therefore there is reasonable ground of linking the PAN Database with Aadhar.

Sec 57 of the Aadhaar Act

"Nothing contained in this Act shall prevent the use of Aadhaar no. for establishing the identity of an individual for any purpose, whether by the Sate or anybody corporate pr person, pursuant to any law, for the time being in force, or any contract to this effect"

It can be used for establishing the identity of an individual 'for any purpose'. Such law should be subjected to judicial scrutiny. This part of provision which enables body corporate between the individual and such body corporate or Persons would impinge upon the Right to Privacy of such individuals.

Filing Returns

Sec 139AA of IT Act makes Aadhaar Mandatory for filing IT Returns and applying for PAN.

As per triple test it was held that linking PAN with Aadhaar will not violate the Right to privacy therefore it was mandatory.

Linking of Bank Accounts

By way of 2017Amendment to Prevention of Money Laundering Act Rules, 2005Linking of Bank Accounts and Other Financial Instruments with Aadhaar were made mandatory.

SC held that it does not stand the proportionality test because just for preventing Money Laundering, there cannot be such a provision targeting every resident as a suspicious person, which is seen as disproportionate. The amendment was declared unconstitutional as it covers banking details and therefore violates the Right to Privacy.

Section 7

According to Section 7 of the Aadhaar Act 2016, any Individual who is desirous of availing any subsidy, Benefit or Services for which the

Expenditure is incurred form.

SC stated that Aadhaar enrolment is of voluntary nature However, it becomes compulsory for those who seeks to receive any subsidy, benefit or service under the welfare scheme of the govt. expenditure whereof is to be met out of consolidated fund of India.

Ratio of the Judgment passed was – 4:1 as Justice D.Y.Chandrachud gave dissenting judgment stating ' The Aadhaar Act, 2016 is declared unconstitutional for failing to meet the necessary requirements to have been certified as a Money Bill under A 110(1). Adequate norms must be laid down for each step from the collection to retention of biometric data based on informed consent, individuals must be given the right to access, correct and delete data. An opt-out option should be necessarily provided.

CHAPTER SEVEN

BIG DATA AND COPYRIGHT

Author: Shubhangi Chhaya, III year of B.A.,LL.B. from Christ (deemed to be) University

INTRODUCTION

According to the Berne Convention, copyright protects literary and artistic works that must first fulfill the "originality" requirement. Depending on the jurisdiction, such works may also have to fulfill the requirement of "fixation" and/or "human intellectual creations[1]".

An original work, in contrast to copies, reproductions, plagiarism, or derivative works, refers to a work created by the author and reflects the author's own intellectual creation. Works, as the object of copyright, are expressions of the author's certain ideas and emotions. The intangibility of the object is the essential characteristic that distinguishes intellectual property rights from other property rights, as does the object of copyright. However, such intangible objects can usually be fixed in a tangible form.

Article 2 of the Berne Convention provides that "it shall; however, be a matter for legislation in the countries of the Union to prescribe that works in general or any specified categories of works shall not be protected unless they have been fixed in some material form[2]."

The TRIPS Agreement recognizes computer software as "literary work" under the Berne Convention[3]. Ordinarily, copyright laws protect software and computer programs used to gather and analyze Big Data. Original data analysis tools used to mine, clean, separate, and transform data can also be copyrighted.

To be eligible for protection, a piece of software and other data analysis tools sought to be protected by copyright must have been reduced into writing or expressed in a fixed medium and must possess some level of originality. In arriving at what constitute "originality", the Berne Convention, states that the Collections of literary or artistic works such as encyclopedias and anthologies which, by reason of the selection and arrangement of their contents, constitute intellectual creations shall be protected as such, without prejudice to the copyright in each of the works forming part of such collections[4].

DEFINING BIG DATA

The origins of large data sets go back to the 1960s and '70s when the world of data was just getting started with the first data centers and the development of the relational database.

Big data refers to data that is so large, fast or complex that it's difficult or impossible to process using traditional methods. The act of accessing and storing large amounts of information for analytics has been around for a long time.

The concept of big data gained momentum in the early 2000s when industry analyst Doug Laney articulated the now-mainstream definition of big data as the three V's[5]-

Volume - Organizations collect data from a variety of sources, including transactions, smart (IoT) devices, industrial equipment, videos, images, audio, social media and more. In the past, storing all that data would have been too costly – but cheaper storage using data lakes, Hadoop and the cloud have eased the burden[6].

Velocity - With the growth in the Internet of Things, data streams into businesses at an unprecedented speed and must be handled in a timely manner. RFID tags, sensors and smart meters are driving the need to deal with these torrents of data in near-real time[7].

Variety - Data comes in all types of formats from structured, numeric data in traditional databases to unstructured text documents, emails, videos, audios, stock ticker data and financial transactions.

Around 2005, people began to realize just how much data users generated through Facebook, YouTube, and other online services. Put simply, big data is larger, more complex data sets, especially from new data sources. These data sets are so voluminous that traditional data processing software just can't manage them. But these massive volumes of data can be used to address business problems you wouldn't have been able to tackle before.

With the advent of the Internet of Things (IoT), more objects and devices are connected to the internet, gathering data on customer usage patterns and product performance[8]. The emergence of machine learning has produced still more data.

Big data is a term that describes large, hard-to-manage volumes of data, both structured and unstructured. But it's not just the type or amount of data that's important, it's what organizations do with the data that matters. Big data can be analyzed for insights that improve decisions and give confidence for making strategic business moves.

DEFINING COPYRIGHT

Intellectual property is defined by the Oxford English Dictionary as "intangible property that is the result of creativity"[9]. Intellectual property rights are the rights that adhere to such creations and that grant the holder thereof a monopoly on the use of that creation for a specified period and subject to certain exceptions.

The underlying aim of granting such (temporary) monopoly, which entails a certain social cost, is to incentivize creators to share their creation with the public, and to achieve the social benefits of increased creative activity.

According to the Berne Convention, copyright protects literary and artistic works that must first fulfill the "originality" requirement[10]. Copyright refers to the legal right of the owner of intellectual property. In simpler terms, copyright is the right to copy. This means that the original creators of products and anyone they give authorization to are the only ones with the exclusive right to reproduce the work.

When someone creates a product that is viewed as original and that required significant mental activity to create, this product becomes an intellectual property that must be protected from unauthorized duplication. Examples of unique creations include computer software, art, poetry, graphic designs, musical lyrics and compositions, novels, film, original architectural designs, website content, etc. One safeguard that can be used to legally protect an original creation is copyright.

RELATION BETWEEN BIG DATA AND COPYRIGHT

Copyright interfaces with Big Data in several aspects. From the computer software applied in data collection and processing to the data sets (collections of data), to the outcomes generated via Big Data technologies.

In the context of big data projects, it is crucial to understand to what extent the data used can be copyright protected. In all likelihood, most of the data collected and processed in a big data analytics context will not be considered original and will therefore not benefit from copyright protection[11]. Having said that, it cannot be excluded that the individual data can gain originality once they are connected with other information or presented in an original way (by means of different possible forms of expression).

Copyright comes into the picture since the law safeguards the computer software and programs that are used to collect and analyze big data. In most countries, such tools are used for data analytics that aid in mining, deleting, segregating, and transforming the data can be protected; for instance, Copyright Laws in Nigeria, India, and the USA[12].

Ordinarily, copyright laws protect software and computer programs used to gather and analyze Big Data. It is important to note that to be eligible for protection, a piece of software and other data analysis tools sought to be protected by copyright must have been reduced into writing or expressed in a fixed medium and must possess some level of originality. In arriving at what constitute "originality", the Berne Convention, states that the "Collections of literary or artistic works such as encyclopedias and anthologies which, by reason of the selection and arrangement of their contents, constitute intellectual creations shall be protected as such, without prejudice to the copyright in each of the works forming part of such collections.[13]"

<u>CASE STUDIES OF BIG DATA AND COPYRIGHT</u>

Data is IP,data is critical to our survival and our competitive edge. Data could reveal something around power density in a fuel cell. That data, if it got into the wrong hands, could result in us losing competitive edge in the market.

"What people don't understand is that data is a commodity now, and that it will be a more valuable commodity than property in the future," Says Shaw Jonathan.[14]

In the Google Books case, the database basically consists of word-searchable scans of the books. From a copyright standpoint, therefore, it is doubtful whether a Big Data corpus of this sort, or a "dump" of personal data scraped from online search engines or social media sites would benefit from copyright protection[15]. Hacking and other methods of unauthorized access to such corpora might be better handled via computer crimes and torts.

Website can plant small pieces of data known as cookies to identify the user, cookies can be used to record the user's browsing activity on that site. These cookies can then be shared and the data therein consolidated to enable the behavioral advertising industry to broadcast, in real time, the usage patterns and interests of the user, and therefore to facilitate real-time bids by online advertisers for personalized advertising on the user's browser page[16].

Netflix implements data analytics models to discover customer behavior and buying patterns. Then, using this information it recommends movies and TV shows to their customers. That is, it analyzes the customer's choice and preferences and suggests shows and movies accordingly.

According to Netflix, around 75% of viewer activity is based on personalized recommendations. Netflix generally collects data, which is enough to create a detailed profile of its subscribers or customers[17]. This profile helps them to know their customers better and in the growth of the business. Google uses big data to optimize and refine its core search and ad-serving algorithms. And Google continually develops new products and services that have big data algorithms.

Google generally uses big data from its Web index to initially match the queries with potentially useful results. It uses machine-learning algorithms to assess the reliability of data and then ranks the sites accordingly[18].

Google optimized its search engine to collect the data from us as we browse the Web and show suggestions according to our preferences and interests.

The leading e-commerce company Amazon, Inc. (Amazon) utilized its big data resources to improve its performance. Being the dominant retailer on the Internet, Amazon had a vast database regarding the tastes, preferences, and previous purchasing history of its customers[19]. Amazon leveraged its big data resources to give more relevant product recommendations and improve its customer care quality. Banking heavily on its big data resources, it upgraded its customer recommendation system.

<u>ANALYSIS</u>

The copyright holder is granted several exclusive economic rights that allow controlling the protected work's use and facilitate enforcement in case a third party uses the work without authorization. The rights of reproduction, communication to the public and distribution are indeed a useful toolkit which, balanced by the copyright exceptions, allows for an optimal protection of right holder's interests.

Copyright law therefore provides for a wide scope of measures securing the rights of the author in case of dissemination of his work and the use of these works by third parties. The rules governing copyright protection aim at enabling further use of the works, securing at the same time the legitimate interests of the author.

For a work to be protected, it must be fixed in some material (concrete) form. In this context, 'fixation', in a data context, would mean that the specific information needs to be saved in a tangible form. The form of saving the data can differ from handwritten notes (files), through photographic documentation (image) or recorded testimonies (sound) to digitized archives (digital files), as long as it remains concrete, can be easily identified and described. Results that have not yet been produced (future data), or results that cannot yet be described (e.g. because there are no means yet to express them) cannot benefit from copyright protection for as long as they have not materialized.

This can present some difficulties in a big data context, given that big data tends to involve dynamic datasets and notably relies on cloud computing services. In a data environment, the most important hindrance resulting from copyright protection is the necessity to obtain authorizations from the copyright holder of each individual data. In the context of big data projects, to the extent copyright applies, it would require identifying authors of hundreds (if not hundreds of thousands) of works. In many cases, it might be difficult to identify or find the right holder and/or understand whether he has given his authorizations for use of the work. In practice, this means that time-consuming analyses need to be performed before the data gathered can be used.

CONCLUSION

In conclusion to all the above discussion a final question emerges that - will big data qualify for copyright protection? The answer that can be concluded from the analysis is since these big data outputs are visualizations of data processing; they can be expressed in a material form. Thus, they meet the "fixation" requirement.

Secondly, it appears that these outputs will possess originality – either as compilations (outcomes of selection and arrangement of raw data according to an algorithm), or as a work of more creativity (articles, poems, painting, etc.).

In addition to this it has to be reconsidered what actually counts as authorship when it comes to big data. After all, the majority of the 'work' involved is undertaken by computing software, thus creating a sizable grey area between human creators and the tools they are using in the digital age.

Thus current IP laws are not adequate to guard precious pools of data available in the digital universe, and legislations have to be made expanding the scope of existing IP laws or developing entirely new IP protection regime.

CHAPTER EIGHT

WHAT DOES PUTIN WANT AND WHERE WILL HE STOP?

Author: Ayushi Tomar, II year of B.A.,LL.B.

Ukraine, a 44-million-strong European democracy, has been assailed by Russia. Its forces are raiding city centers and shutting in on the Ukrainian capital,Kyiv, causing a massive evacuation.

The Ukrainian country is already at war with Russia and the answers to all the Ukraine-Russia crisis lies in history, and why Vladimir Putin is so obsessiveabout Ukraine.

There was a time when Kyiv was more powerful than Moscow; when Ukraine and America were adversaries, and was crucial strategically, economically, and culturally.

We will get down to the ninth century. There was a state called Kievan Rus, where the Slavic people lived, with Kyivas the capital. Between 980 and 1085, the Kievan Rus was ruled by Grand Prince Volodymir. In Russian, his name is Vladimir, in Ukrainian – Volodymir; and as fate would have it, these are also the names of the presidents of these countries today. Anyways, Russians and Ukrainians draw their lineage from this Slavic state. Plenty has changed in the centuries that followed.The shared inheritance of the countrieshas been used for electoral and military goals.

Ukraine was under Russian rule. In the 1900s, the two were soviet republics: Russian- the most powerful of the 15 republicans and Ukraine – the second most powerful. It had defense industries, large agricultural lands and housed much of the soviet nuclear arsenal. During the cold war, Ukraine was the chief opponent of the United States.

The USSR collapsed in 1991; Ukraine became independent, as did Russia. Ukraine inherited much of the Soviet arsenal but gave it up to Russia in 1994. In exchange, Moscow guaranteed Ukraine's security and promised to respect its sovereignty. They signed the Budapest Memorandum along with Belarus, Kazakhstan, the U.K, and the U.S.

Cut to November 2013, Viktor Yanukovych was the president of Ukraine, who had a reputation for heavy-handedness, corruption, and specifically, for being openly pro-Moscow. In 2013, he rejected the EU trade deal, which could have meant greater integration with European Union; instead,Yanukovych decided to take a $15 billion bailout from Russia. To many Ukrainians, it felt like being traded in with Moscow, so, protests broke out. They were called 'EUROMAIDAN': 'Euro' because these protests were about Europe and 'Maidan' because they happened in Kyiv's Maidan Nezalezhnosti what we today know as the Independence Square. Here protesters chanted, "sign the EU deal", "Yanukovych must step down". Russia supported the president, and the west supported the protesters. In February 2014, Yanukovych's government was toppled, the president was oustedfrom Ukraine, who then fled to Russia. Not the whole of Ukraine waspleased with this, Russian-speaking east wanted Yanukovych to stay. When he was ejected, the minority felt disenfranchised. Yanukovych's ejection made Russia vexed as it has lost its pawn and to reclaim its ball game, Moscow annexed Crimea, and why Crimea?

Crimea is a peninsula located in the Black Sea, in Eastern Europe. In 1954, Nikita Khrushchev, a communist of the Soviet Union, handed over Crimea from Russian Soviet Socialist Republic to the Ukrainian Soviet Socialist Republic. Why? Khrushchev hoped this transfer would strengthen the ties between Russia and Ukraine, he says and I quote, "Brotherly ties between the Ukrainian and the Russian people". When Ukraine became independent in 1991, the peninsulawas made part of it and was given special autonomy, thoughit remained home to the Russian Military bases with Moscow assuring to respect Crimean autonomy. Many in Russia were of the opinion that Crimea should not have been allowed to join Ukraine. In 2014, when Yanukovych was driven out from power in Ukraine, the Russian military began seizing government buildings in Crimea. So, the entire peninsula was under military occupation. A referendum followed, and on the 16th of March 2014, Crimea voted to become a part of Russia. Was this vote legitimate? Well, it depends on who you ask. For Putin this was Crimea's liberation, but, for the rest of the world, it was considered

Crimea's annexation.Also, to mention, Russians have an interest in the black sea too.The Black Sea region's distinct topography provides Russia with significant geopolitical advantages. For starters, it serves as a crucial crossroads and key intersection for the entire region. All bordering states require access to the Black Sea, which considerably boosts power projection into various adjacent regions.Second, the region is an important transportation station for manufacture and energy.

In April 2014, the focus was shifted to eastern Ukraine, where Russia backed the separatists, who began seizing territory in eastern Ukraine.Since 2014, a pro-Russian separatist movement has been operating in eastern Ukraine's Donbas area which is deliberately supported by the Russian government. Ukrainian forces did not launch an all-out offensive at first but on the 17th of July 2014, when the flight carrying 298 was shot down by these rebels, Ukrainian forces decided to flush out the rebels. The Separatists were deteriorating so the Russian army intervened. They invaded eastern Ukraine and fought next to the rebels. A series of talks between Russia, Ukraine, and the west ensued and resulted in the Minsk accords. Minsk agreement was first signed in 2014. Both sides agreed to ceasefire and military withdrawal; Ukraine agreed to hold elections in rebel-held areas. Eight years on, Minsk Accords remained unimplemented.

Ukraine stands as the largest European country, after Russia. It encompasses an area of more than 600,000 square kilometers, with a population of 44 million; a GDP of more than $155 billion, per capita income of more than $3700. Today Ukraine is divided into the east and the west, in more ways than one. The west sees itself as more European, the east is close to Russia, be it in terms of geography or sentiments; in the west, most Ukrainians speak Ukrainian while in the east, a-third are native Russians; in the west, Russia is looked at with suspicion; in the east, Russia is looked at through the lens of shared history and heritage.Ukraine remains at war in and out. Its forces are fighting rebels in the east; rebel leaders are ruling at least two regions, Donetsk and Luhansk- together they are known as the Donbas region. Russia has once again sent its troops and this time; they are stationed at the border.

<u>What does Putin want?</u>

Putin wants NATO to stop expanding. NATO stands for North Atlantic Treaty Organization. It is a military alliance. In 1949, there were 12 founding members of the Alliance: Belgium, Canada, Denmark, France, Iceland, Italy, Luxembourg, the Netherlands, Norway,Portugal, theUnited

Kingdom, and the United States. At present, NATO has 30 members. Ukraine wants to join NATO too but Putin wants NATO to exclude Ukraine and every other former Soviet State.

And this is just half of the story, a lot is hidden in history. For starters, there is domestic politics. When Putin annexed Crimea, his approval ratings sky-rocketed: "Almost nine out of ten Russians approve their President, according to survey and that also highlights support for Ukraine strategy." Keeping the nationalistic drum rolling helps the Russian president. Annexing parts of Ukraine also helps Putin to restore Russia's superpower image. Having a glimpse of history again, many Russians view Ukraine's independence as a mistake. It is true, Ukraine was ruled by Russia. In fact, Ukraine has barely remained independent pre-1991. There was a brief period in World War I, and then another stint in 1600. For the rest of its modern history, Ukraine was under Russia; one in six Ukrainians is an ethnic Russian; one in three speaks Russian as a native language, so, Putin is right when he says, "Historically, we are one." But claiming Ukraine on basis of colonial history is wrong. It will be like, Britain claiming India or South Africa, or, Spain claiming the Philippines. "Past-imperialism cannot justify present-day expansionism."

History tells us that Ukraine was forcefully Russified. Cut to 1700, the Russian leader Katherine, the Great, started Russifying Ukraine; ethnic Russians were shifted to this part of the world; schools were instructed to teach the Russian language; by 1800, the Ukrainian language was banned. In 1930, Soviet leader Joseph Stalin steered a famine in Ukraine; millions of Ukrainians were killed and the area was then, repopulated with ethnic Russians. In the 1940s, the ethnic Tatars were relocated, who were, too, replaced with Russians. There is a reason today why eastern Ukraine has so many native Russian speakers. It was designed to be that way. Eastern Ukraine was always dear to Russia- it has coal, it has iron, fertile land. Its historical connection with Russia was forced. Putin, time and again, talks about the 'HOLY RUS'. He says, "Russians and Ukrainians are one people." And what do Ukrainians feel about Putin's view?

- Seventy-one percent of Ukrainians reject this thought.
- Seventy-two percent consider Russia as a hostile state.
- 33.3% of Ukrainians are ready to take up arms against Russia.
- 31.7% are ready to stage civil resistance against Russia.
- 67% of the Ukrainians want to join the EU.

- 59% want to join NATO.

The Ukrainian President Volodymyr Zelensky, came to power in 2019, following a landslide victory. He is a vocal critic of Russia. Zelensky openly opposes the Russian occupation of eastern Ukraine.73% percent of Ukrainian voters voted this man to power. Today, Zelensky represents the pulse of Ukraine, the Ukraine which wants to remain independent of Russia. But Vladimir Putin wants to become the man who revived Russian imperialism. He does not realize the world has moved on.

<u>ARE WE ON THE VERGE OF THE WORLD WAR III?</u>

143 countries vote against Russia at the United Nations for Russia to end the invasion of Ukraine. The United Nations says, "More than a million people have fled Ukraine." Where did they go? Poland, Germany, Romania, Belarus, Slovakia, Russia. With every passing day, this war is becoming bigger and pulling in more countries. Is this World War III? Are we on the brink of World War 3? The day Russia invaded Ukraine World War 3 was trending on Twitter. So, let's place the current war against the definition and checklist set by history- 'a World War is a war that involves the whole world or, at least the majority of it.' In World War I, for example,between 1914 and 1918, more than 100 countries from Africa, the Americas, Asia, Australasia, and Europe were part of the conflict. As we speak, only Ukraine and Russia are fighting, the rest of the countries are not on the frontline. So, history won't agree if we call the war in Ukraine, a world war. but here is something else that history tells us- World war often starts small. Flashback 1914, on the 28th of June, Archduke Franz Ferdinand, the heir to the Astro-Hungarian Empire, was assassinated in Bosnia by a Serbian Nationalist.The assassination triggered a chain of events that resulted in war between Austria-Hungary and Serbia. Initially, only these two countries were at war, but due to the European alliance system, all the European major countries were drawn into the war and spreading around the whole of the globe. But it all began with just two countries and one assassination. What about the second world war? Flashback to 1939, Germany invades Poland on the 1st of September, two days later, Britain and France declare war on Germany. Once again it was a domino effect, and before you know it, the whole world is fighting and at least 50 million people are dead. It began just with one country invading the other.

So, outbreaks need not be massive for a war to pull in more countries, even a war between two countries can escalate and become a world war.

World wars have clear alliances, prominent countries are divided. WWI had the triple entente and the triple alliance. The entente had France, Russia, and Britain; the alliance had Germany, Austria-Hungary, and Italy. WWII had the axis powers (Germany, Italy, and Japan) and the allies (France. Britain, the United States, and the Soviet Union). At a glance, it appears that only two countries are fighting but if you zoom out, you will see the divided world, each country has picked aside. The United Nations General Assembly held an emergency vote calling for the withdrawal of Russian troops from Ukraine.141 countries voted in favor of this resolution, the list includes the United States, the United Kingdoms, Canada, and Australia; four countries voted in favor of Russia: Belarus, North Korea, Syria, and Eritrea; 35 countries abstained, the countries that decided not to take sides, to not get involved in a war that is neither of their making nor theirs to fight.

America was too in a similar position during the first world war. Initially, it remained neutral,but then American interests started bleeding. Itentered the war on the side of the Allied powers (the United Kingdom, France, and Russia).In 1915, the German aggression escalated, Germany sank British ocean liners carrying hundreds of Americans on board. In 1917, German submarines sank three US merchant ships. There was a heavy loss of life. The then US President Woodrow Wilson decided to declare war on Germany. Back to the war in Ukraine, on the 2nd of March, an Indian student was killed in Ukraine, the same day Slovenia's consulate building in Kharkiv was bombed. The next day, Sweden accused Russia of space violation;on the 4th of March, Russia put the entire continent in danger by attacking a nuclear power plant. Will countries be left with no option but to join this war if their own people continue bleeding? NATO is already prepared for an escalating. It has beefed up deployment in eastern Europe, but France maintains to be not at war with Russia, at least not yet, but French President Emmanuel Macron has declared that the worst is yet to come. What exactly will the worst look like? Will it be a large-scale European conflict? Will there be a wider armed conflict including countries from around the world?

Our world is already fighting multiple wars. Experts say China's conflict with Taiwan will turn into a military conflict sometimes in thenear-decade. China is also fighting multiple countries in the South China Sea, the Philippines, Vietnam, Malaysia, Brunei. India and China are caught in a standoff. There is a conflict between Iran and Israel; Iran and the US; the US and North Korea are arch enemies, so are the US and Cuba. There is also a war in Syria, a war in Yemen, Israel and Palestine are fresh out of a bloody battle, the United Arab Emirates was recently hit by a missile. It is hard to rule out that countries or non-state actors will cease on a distracted world and pursue their geopolitical dreams. It is hard to rule out that an escalation on the side-lines of Ukraine will drag in more countries. It is also hard to rule out that the war in Ukraine itself will intensify and swallow more nations.

Sergei Lavrov, Russia's foreign minister says, "it is clear that World War three can only be nuclear." Nine countries are said to have nuclear weapons today: the US, Pakistan, India, Israel, and North Korea. In total, there are 13,000 weapons, enough and more to wipe out our world. Russia has put its nuclear deterrent team on alert.

The world cannot afford to go to war. One cannot be sure what lies ahead. Is this a prelude to World War III? Is this cold war II? When asked to Joe Biden if it'sa cold war, "it depends", he says, "from where I'm sitting, I see ample signs of a new cold war. There are two clear sides: one led by Russia and the other by the US. Then there are countries that have chosen to stay out. There is talk of possible world war or signs of an escalating conflict and I see a President who refuses to back down. Well, one thing is for sure, whichever side our world swings, we are entering an entirely new era of geopolitics."

www.ingramcontent.com/pod-product-compliance
Lightning Source LLC
Chambersburg PA
CBHW051335150726
47997CB00004B/1471